My Family

by Mario García

 NATIONAL GEOGRAPHIC

 Hampton-Brown

National Geographic and the Yellow Border are registered trademarks of the National Geographic Society.

WCN: 01-100-414

National Geographic School Publishing
Hampton-Brown
www.NGSP.com

ISBN: 978-0-7362-7985-7

Print Number: 6   Print Year: 2024
Printed in Mexico

Acknowledgments and credits continue on the inside back cover.

mother

Who is this? This is my mother.

father

Who is this? This is my father.

sister

Who is this? This is my sister.

brother **brother**

Who is this? This is my brother.

grandma

Who is this? This is my grandma.

grandpa

Who is this? This is my grandpa.

This is my family!

Where is he now?

No, he is in the restaurant.

Where is he?
Is he in the library?

No, he is in the grocery store.

Where is he?
Is he in the post office?

No, he is in the bakery.

Where is he?
Is he in the store?

Where Is He?

by Carlos Santiano

NATIONAL GEOGRAPHIC

Hampton-Brown

National Geographic and the Yellow Border are registered trademarks of the National Geographic Society.

National Geographic School Publishing
Hampton-Brown
www.NGSP.com

Printed in Mexico

ISBN: 978-0-7362-7994-9

Print Number: 10   Print Year: 2020

Acknowledgments and credits continue on the inside back cover.